The 100th Meridian Initiative:

A Strategic Approach to Prevent the Westward Spread of Zebra Mussels and Other Aquatic Nuisance Species

I0435024

Prepared by:
Susan Mangin
Division of Fish and Wildlife Management Assistance
U.S. Fish and Wildlife Service

Endorsed by:
The Western Regional Panel

cover Zebra mussel illustration: Rick Hill

Table of Contents

Acknowledgments

This Initiative is based on an action plan, developed by the Western Regional Panel, to prevent the spread of aquatic nuisance species (ANS) west of the 100th meridian (*The 100th Meridian Initiative - Draft Action Plan*, January 1998). The basic tenets of the action plan have been expanded and refined through the cooperative efforts of numerous dedicated biologists and managers, many of whom are the front line defense for combating ANS in the west. Their experience, knowledge, and vision ensure that implementation of this Initiative will help prevent the spread of zebra mussels and other ANS into the west.

In particular, I would like to thank Gary Edwards and Robert Peoples who were the driving forces behind this Initiative. Their concern about the impact that zebra mussels and other ANS could have on native ecosystems and manmade structures in the west motivated them to guide this project to completion. Hannibal Bolton provided unwavering support for this project and directed my work load so that the majority of my time was dedicated to developing and completing this project.

Finally, I would like to recognize Linda Drees, Bob Pitman, and Kim Webb. Their professionalism and dedication to preventing, controlling, and eradicating ANS has been an inspiration. Their willingness to share insights and suggestions relative to this Initiative has been invaluable. It has been a tremendous pleasure working with all those who contributed to this Initiative.

Executive Summary

Zebra mussels are prolific alien invaders that have rapidly become established in waters of the eastern United States and Canada. These natives of the Black, Caspian, Azov and Aral Sea drainage basins were first discovered in Lake St. Clair near Detroit, Michigan, in 1988. By 1991, they had spread throughout the Great Lakes basin and are now established throughout the Mississippi River basin and are spreading west into Oklahoma. Except for Oklahoma, zebra mussels have not been detected in open waters of the West. However, without effective prevention measures, their invasion into the West is a real and imminent possibility.

Zebra mussels are causing significant economic and ecological impacts throughout their range. They have biofouled thousands of municipal and industrial water delivery systems, resulting in annual expenditures of up to several $100,000 for control and detection activities. They are significantly impacting aquatic ecosystems, altering nutrient flow, decimating native mussel populations, and providing a sink for environmental contaminants.

The major pathway for zebra mussels to invade the West is not from the ballast water of ships but from boats, personal watercraft, and related equipment transported from infested to uninfested waters. Zebra mussels attach to hulls, trailers, and other exposed locations on boats, boating equipment, and personal watercraft. Their free-living larva can enter motors, live wells, or other moist areas and may remain viable for more than 10 days when attached to boat hulls (Tyus, Dwyer, and Whitmore 1993). Their adaptability, their lack of natural predators, and the propensity of boaters to move their boats from one body of water to another have facilitated the rapid spread of zebra mussels throughout their current range.

Additional pathways for the spread of zebra mussels and other ANS are also a major concern for western States and Tribes and public and private entities. These other pathways must be addressed, but formulating plans to deal with them will take time and resources. Consequently, this Initiative's primary focus is on the transfer of zebra mussels and other ANS through recreational activities and commercial boat hauling. Additional pathways will be addressed as resources permit.

Amendments to Public Law 101-636 call for the development of a program to prevent the spread of zebra mussels west of the 100th meridian. This 100th Meridian Initiative outlines management activities that will help prevent, detect, and control zebra mussels and other ANS in 100th meridian jurisdictions and west. The 100th meridian jurisdictions include Texas, Oklahoma, Kansas, Nebraska, North and South Dakota, and Manitoba.

The goals of the 100th Meridian Initiative are to: 1) prevent the spread of zebra mussels and other ANS in the 100th meridian jurisdictions and west and 2) monitor and control zebra mussels and other ANS if detected in these areas. These goals will be achieved by addressing seven components: 1) information and education, 2) voluntary boat inspections and boater surveys, 3) commercially hauled boats, 4) monitoring, 5) rapid response, 6) identification and risk assessment of additional pathways, and 7) evaluation.

The 100th Meridian Initiative represents the first comprehensive and strategically focused effort, involving Federal, State, Tribal and Provincial entities, potentially affected industries, and other interested parties to begin addressing pathways to prevent the westward spread of zebra mussels and other ANS. Success will depend on the commitment and support of these groups to aggressively combat the introduction and spread of these destructive invaders.

I. Background

A. Dispersal

Zebra mussels (*Dreissena polymorpha*) are indigenous to the Aral, Caspian, Azov, and Black Seas. In the 19th century, zebra mussels invaded northern European rivers that empty into the Black Sea (Karnaukhov and Karnaukhov 1993). They became dispersed throughout Europe by barges once the canal system became connected over 200 years ago. By 1930, they had spread into Great Britain. Since the early 1920's, scientists postulated that zebra mussels could be spread to the United States through shipping (Nalepa and Schlosser 1993).

Zebra mussels were first discovered in Lake St. Claire in the Great Lakes region in 1988. They probably arrived in the ballast water of vessels originating from Europe. They rapidly spread and by 1992 were found in all five Great Lakes. They have now spread throughout the Mississippi River drainage as far south as New Orleans and as far west as the Arkansas River in Oklahoma. They have also spread eastward into the Hudson River drainage and Lake Champlain.

Attaching to ships and barges has been a major pathway by which zebra mussels have become dispersed throughout the Great Lakes and the Mississippi River basin. Other pathways such as waterways flowing between infested and uninfested areas, trailered boats, personal watercraft, aquaculture activities, the aquatic plant aquarium trade, and fishing gear and bait have also contributed to their distribution.

Zebra mussels' ability to spread by attaching themselves to boats, personal watercraft, and related equipment is a major concern because they can remain viable under adverse environmental conditions. Adults can live out of water for up to 10 days if they are in shaded humid areas. Boats spending as little as 1 or 2 days in infested water can carry zebra mussels on their hulls, engine drive units, and anchor chains. Zebra mussel larvae can be carried in boat bilge water, live wells, bait buckets, and engine cooling water systems even if the boat has been in infested water for only a short time (New York Sea Grant Extension Fact Sheet 1994).

Conditions leading to the initial dispersion for zebra mussels in the East do not exist for western waters. Specifically, transport on boats and barges in western tributaries of the Mississippi River is constrained by relatively short navigable reaches and limited riverine traffic. In addition, those areas flow away from the area of concern. Also, environmental conditions in the arid and semiarid West may aid in deterring the spread of zebra mussels.

The primary pathways for the western spread of zebra mussels will be through their transport on recreational boats, associated equipment, and personal watercraft. A survey conducted at the U.S/Canada border of boaters and boats in watersheds that contribute to surface water in Manitoba produced alarming results. Ninety-three percent of the boats originated from jurisdictions with waters containing zebra mussels, 5% had been in waters with zebra mussels within the past 5 days, 60% had been drained, and only 32% had been cleaned since boating in zebra mussel infested waters (Fish Futures, Inc. 1994). A separate survey was conducted for boats entering Glen Canyon National Recreation Area in Utah. Results indicate that numerous boats entering Lake Powell were from areas infested with zebra mussels (National Park Service information).

Zebra mussel transfer via trailered boats is a real threat. Inspectors from California's Department of Food and Agriculture have found both live and dead zebra mussels on 18 trailered boats transported into the State from the fall of 1993 until the spring of 1999 (California Department of Food and Agriculture).

B. Biology and Life History

Zebra mussels vary morphologically, hence the species name "polymorpha" meaning many forms. Although most have jagged lateral black or brown stripes, some have longitudinal bands while others are totally cream or black (Marsden 1992). They can grow up to 2 inches in length but most are under an inch (see Figure 1).

Figure 1. Zebra Mussels (Don Schloesser)

Zebra mussels mature between 12 to 18 months under favorable conditions and can spawn more than once annually. One female can produce over 1 million eggs per season (Miller et al. 1992). Fertilized eggs become free swimming larvae (veligers) that eventually attach to hard surfaces and develop into hard-shelled juvenile mussels (post veligers). Preferred substrates include stone, wood, concrete, iron/steel, aluminum, plastics, and fiberglass (O'Neill 1996). As many as 700,000 post veligers/m^2 have settled in raw water systems during one spawning season (Miller et al. 1992; McMahon et al. 1993). They have formed mats up to 12-inches thick (Tyus, Dwyer, and Whitmore 1993).

Zebra mussels spread rapidly to different areas and thus are also called the "wandering mussel" (Nalepa and Schloesser 1993). They can drop their attachments (byssal threads) and move to other locations and then regenerate threads to reattach. They form buoyant strands that allow them to drift with the currents. Zebra mussels can also use their muscular foot to move (Tyus, Dwyer, and Whitmore, 1993). Zebra mussels have been found in water as deep as 180 feet but most often occur at depths between 6 to 12 feet (Mackie, et al. 1989).

C. Economic Impacts

Zebra mussels are having devastating economic effects on municipal and residential drinking water delivery systems, power plant intakes, and industrial facilities that use raw surface water. They biofoul water delivery systems beginning at the site of water intake and then multiply throughout the facility (O'Neill 1996) (see Figure 2).

Figure 2. Zebra Mussels Fouling Pipe (Don Schloesser)

Zebra mussel layers greater than 0.3 meters have been found in intake mains of some Great Lakes facilities. A 1- to 2-mm layer of zebra mussels throughout a pipeline can reduce water-carrying efficiency by 5% to 10% due to increased friction. Unlike saltwater or estuarine raw water systems, most inland raw water systems are generally not designed to deal with macrofouling organisms. Screens used to prevent fish impingement or to remove debris allow zebra mussel veligers to pass, resulting in the colonization of the facility's raw water piping system (O'Neill 1996).

Biofouling of conduits results in head loss and increased pumping resistance. Tubing may become clogged, ultimately leading to components overheating. Zebra mussels can clog service and water lines and can damage vital plant components or cause safety hazards if the flow for fire control systems is impeded (*ibid*).

Due to their filtration activities, they may not leave enough particulate matter to provide effective coagulation at water treatment plants. This may require the plant to change its treatment technology, increasing operating costs. In addition, as zebra mussels selectively feed on green algae, an increased portion of blue-green algae is present. This may cause water to have a foul taste and odor, also increasing treatment costs (*ibid*).

Controlling zebra mussels is costly. Results of a 1995 study indicated that between 1988 and 1995 facilities expended over $69 million in zebra mussel-related expenses such as monitoring and control (O'Neill 1995). A paper company spent $1.4 million to remove 400 cubic yards of zebra mussels from its intake in Lake Michigan (USGS 1997). In Ontario, Canada, the costs of preventing zebra mussel infestations at 8 hydro power facilities, 86 municipal plants, and 67 industrial plants were over $172 million. To control zebra mussels in the Great Lakes, small and large volume water users may annually spend $20,000 and $460,000, respectively (Indiana DNR).

D. Boating Impacts

Zebra mussels biofoul boat hulls causing surface damage and increasing drag, which increases fuel costs. Boat motors are also affected and can become overheated due to clogged water inlets. Although antifouling paints may prevent zebra mussels from building up on hulls, their use is banned or restricted in some States because of adverse effects on other aquatic organisms.

E. Ecological Impacts

Habitat loss is the primary cause for the decline in native mussels. However, zebra mussels have added a new threat. Zebra mussels often attach around the gape of native mussels, preventing them from opening and closing their valves (see Figure 3). They may even cover the native mussel's entire surface and then begin settling on top of each other. (Mackie, 1989).

Figure 3. Zebra Mussels Attached to Native Mussel (Don Schloesser)

Zebra mussels also compete with native mussels for food, which may be responsible for the community-wide unionid decrease in some areas in the East. In Lake Erie, mean densities of 6,777 zebra mussels per native mussel were found (Schloesser and Kovalak 1991).

An adult zebra mussel can filter about one liter of water per day. These filtering activities increase water clarity allowing deeper light penetration, encouraging the growth of benthic organisms. Zebra mussels have increased the water clarity of Lake Erie up to 600% and reduced some types of phytoplankton by up to 80% (Sea Grant Great Lakes Network 1998).

F. Potential Impacts

The establishment of zebra mussels west of the 100th meridian could devastate water resource projects, raw water users, and aquatic ecosystems. If zebra mussels become established in headwater reservoirs, they would likely inhabit/colonize thousands of canals used to transport this water. This infested water would also be pumped to agricultural and municipal areas, thus spreading the mussels over large areas in a relatively short time. In lower elevations and wetter climates, surface water could become contaminated from waters originating at higher elevations. Once this water is transported to downstream receiving areas, they too would become infested (Tyus, Dwyer, and Whitmore 1993).

Although the western most point of the zebra mussel invasion is the Arkansas River in Oklahoma, there is increasing concern that they could severely impact western economies and ecology if they invade further west. For example, if zebra mussels invaded California, they could negatively impact hundreds of reservoirs, thousands of miles of steel and concrete pipes and canals, water gates and intakes, fish screens, filter plants, agricultural irrigation systems, and other water delivery system components. A large portion of California's population depends on the State Water Project and the Central Valley Project to deliver their water from upstream sources. These water management projects with their shallow, warm canals could provide optimal chemical and physical conditions for zebra mussels. If zebra mussels become established in areas such as the Sacramento/San Joaquin delta, they could eliminate populations of rare aquatic species, change biotic communities' composition, and change the physical and chemical conditions of aquatic habitats.

In a study of 160 potential sites for zebra mussel establishment in California, 44% had a high potential, 2% had a moderate potential, and 54% had low or no potential for colonization (Cohen and Weinstein 1998). Waters conducive to zebra mussel establishment included facilities such as the Delta-Mendota Canal, the California and South Bay Aqueducts, the Los Angeles Aqueduct, the Colorado River Aqueduct, the All American Canal, and associated reservoirs.

Zebra mussel infestations could increase the Central Arizona Project operations and maintenance costs between $4 and $5 million annually. This does not include the costs to customers, farmers, and water treatment plants (Dreissena! 1998). Water delivered in the west by the Bureau of Reclamation is utilized by farmers to provide the annual food requirements of 38 million people. These water deliveries can be adversely affected by the presence of zebra mussels and other ANS, resulting in maintenance costs in the 10's of millions of dollars.

II. Preventing the Westward Spread

In an effort to prevent the western invasion of zebra mussels, the 1996 amendments to the Nonindigenous Aquatic Nuisance Prevention and Control Act of 1990 (Act) require the Western Regional Panel (Panel) (established by the Act) to make recommendations to the Aquatic Nuisance Species Task Force (Task Force) "regarding an education, monitoring (includes inspection), prevention, and control program to prevent the spread of the zebra mussel west of the 100th meridian." The 100th Meridian Initiative is in response to that requirement (see Figure 4).

The Panel was established under Section 1203 of the Act and is comprised of representatives from western Federal, State, Tribal, and local agencies, and private and commercial interests. The basis for the 100th Meridian Initiative was an action plan developed by the Panel that recognized the significance of trailered boats as a pathway and the special circumstances impeding the westward spread of zebra mussels. The Panel submitted the 100th Meridian Initiative to the Task Force for review and approval.

The Task Force, established under Section 1201 of the Act, is comprised of Federal agencies and ex-officio members. The Task Force, chaired by the U.S. Fish and Wildlife Service and the National Oceanic and Atmospheric Administration, is responsible for the development and implementation of a program to prevent introduction and dispersal of ANS; to monitor, control, and study such species; and to disseminate related information. Upon approval of the 100th Meridian Initiative by the Task Force, Federal funding may be available to cost share with other sources to support implementation.

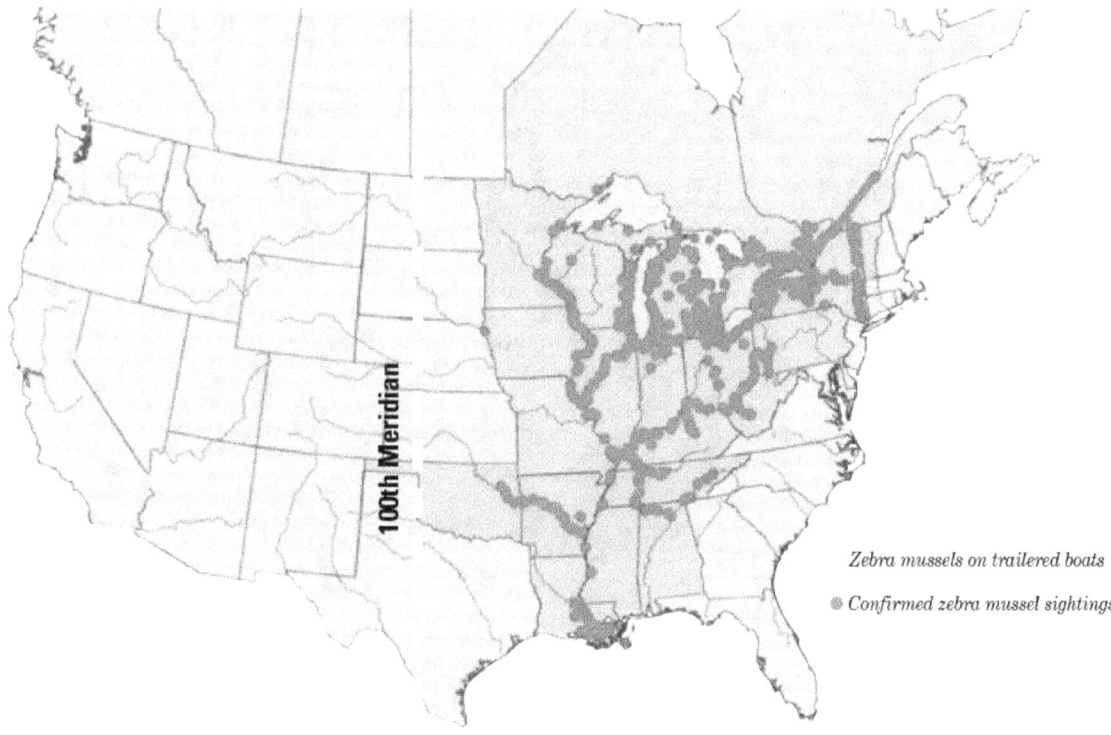

Zebra mussels on trailered boats

● *Confirmed zebra mussel sightings*

Figure 4. Zebra Mussel Sightings (1999 U.S. Geological Survey Map with 100th Meridian Added)

III. The Initiative

The 100th Meridian Initiative is a unique program involving a wide range of partners who are integral in preventing the westward spread of zebra mussels and other ANS. The Initiative's goals are attainable through the combined effort of these partners and implementation of the following components.

Goals and Components

The goals of the 100th Meridian Initiative are to **1) prevent the spread of zebra mussels and other ANS in the 100th meridian jurisdictions and west and 2) monitor and control zebra mussels and other ANS if detected in these areas.** Seven components will be addressed to achieve these goals.

1) **Information and Education:** Inform and educate the public about the ecological and economic impacts of zebra mussels, the pathways by which they spread, and what actions can be taken to prevent their spread.

2) **Voluntary Boat Inspections and Boater Surveys:** Prevent the spread of zebra mussels in the 100th meridian jurisdictions and west through voluntary boat inspections and boater surveys (see Appendix).

3) **Commercially Hauled Boats:** Prevent the spread of zebra mussels in the 100th meridian jurisdictions and west by boats being hauled commercially and/or for professional fishing tournaments.

4) **Monitoring:** Establish monitoring sites on waters in the 100th meridian jurisdictions and west to determine if zebra mussels and other ANS are present.

5) **Rapid Response:** Eradicate or contain zebra mussels immediately following detection.

6) **Identification and Risk Assessment of Additional Pathways:** Establish a program to identify additional pathways by which zebra mussels and other ANS could be introduced west of the 100th meridian. Evaluate these pathways and develop an action plan for those having potential risks.

7) **Evaluation:** Ensure the effectiveness of the 100th Meridian Initiative in preventing the westward spread of zebra mussels and other ANS.

Component I
Information and Education

Objective: Inform and educate the public about the ecological and economic impacts of zebra mussels, the pathways by which they spread, and what actions can be taken to prevent their spread.

This component builds on current efforts directed at preventing the spread of zebra mussels by recreational water activities such as boating and using personal watercraft. Component elements will focus on the detrimental effects of zebra mussels; the impacts of transporting them in or on recreational boats, related equipment, or personal watercraft; and the steps necessary to avoid transport to uninfested waters. Recreationalists using infested waters east of the 100th meridian and those trailering boats or personal watercraft from the east to areas west of the 100th meridian will be targeted. Information will be disseminated through numerous means including print and electronic news coverage, public service announcements, billboards, articles in boating and fishing magazines, talks to sportsmen clubs, posters and brochures placed at marinas and boat landings, and brochures packaged with boating and fishing licenses.

As boaters using major highways approach the 100th meridian from the east, the zebra mussel message will become more intense. Posters and brochures identifying the problem and detailing the inspection and survey process will be placed prominently in rest areas and at restaurants, motels, and gas stations at interchanges. Key messages will be displayed on billboards and highway signs along the 11 targeted interstate highway corridors. Just prior to reaching the inspection sites, highway signs and short-range radio announcements will inform travelers of the inspection and survey sites and urge their participation.

Tasks required to implement this component include:
1) Complete development of a theme, brochure, poster, and sticker describing the Initiative. (This task has been completed.)
2) Print 500,000 brochures.
3) Produce 2,500 posters.
4) Produce 100,000 stickers.
5) Place and replenish brochures and posters at visitor centers, weigh stations, and rest areas west of the Mississippi River.
6) Produce and erect billboards to be used on 11 highway corridors.
7) Develop and print zebra mussel advisory signs.
8) Post zebra mussel advisory signs at public water access sites west of the Mississippi River.
9) Create TV and radio public information spots on preventative messages including inspections.
10) Broadcast spots on radio and TV.
11) Attend boating and sportfishing shows to advertise the Initiative.
12) Place Initiative information in State boater registration packages and fishing regulations when feasible.
13) Develop articles for newspapers and magazines.

Component II
Voluntary Boat Inspections and Boaters Surveys

Objective: Prevent the spread of zebra mussels in the 100th meridian jurisdictions and west through voluntary boat inspections and boater surveys.

Trained personnel will conduct voluntary boat inspections and boater surveys at highway stops located on 11 major highway corridors entering the 100th meridian jurisdictions and at marinas and launch ramps at selected lakes in States west of the 100th meridian. These selected highways are: US2, I-94, US12, I-90, I-80, I-70, US54, I-40, I-20, I-10, and I-44 (see Figure 5). Locations for highway inspections will include weigh stations, highway rest areas/welcome centers, restaurant/service/motel complexes on interchanges, and retailers. Inspections will target boats, trailers, and associated equipment such as anchors and anchor lines. Boaters will be surveyed to learn where their boat has been, what is their destination, etc. (see Appendix). Boaters will receive a brochure explaining the Initiative and what actions they can take to prevent the spread of zebra mussels.

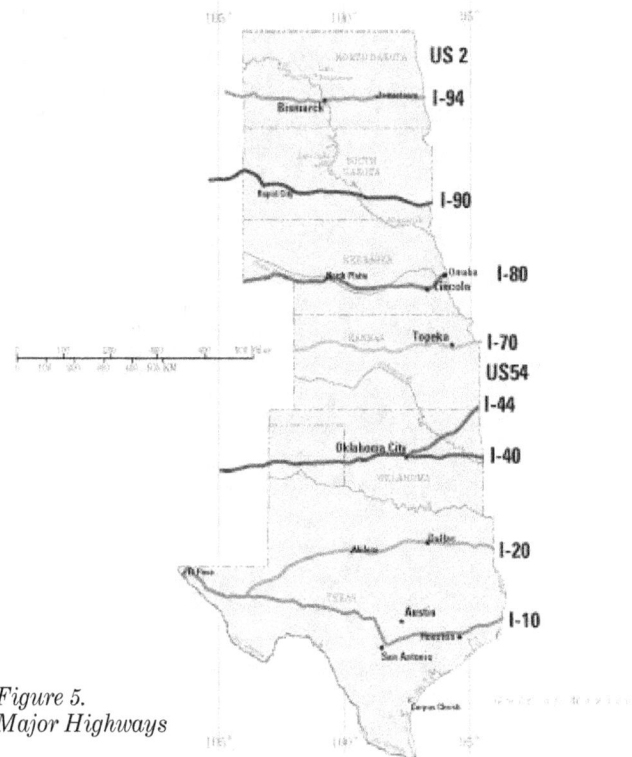

Figure 5.
Major Highways

Data will be collected using the boat inspections and surveys and other unobtrusive means such as counting the number of boats that passed by inspection stations without stopping. Additional data including the number, types, and timing of boats being trailered on each highway corridor and why boaters declined to have their boats inspected will be collected. In addition, State and provincial transportation departments will be asked to develop data to expand the information collected at inspection sites by identifying trailered boats in ongoing State vehicle surveys. Inspection and survey results will be sent for processing to the USFWS, 500 Gold Avenue, S.W., Albuquerque, NM 87102, Attn: Bob Pitman.

These data will be analyzed to include unit costs of various activities. The cost effectiveness of alternative education and information approaches and the adequacy of education efforts alone, in the absence of inspections, will be assessed. These data will be used to evaluate the effectiveness of the 100th Meridian Initiative.

Tasks required to implement this component include:
1) Develop standard inspection procedures.
2) Hire and train boat inspectors.
3) Develop, reproduce, and disseminate inspection and survey forms.
4) Submit completed forms to the Service.

Component III
Commercially Hauled Boats

Objective: Prevent the spread of zebra mussels in the 100th meridian jurisdictions and west by boats being hauled commercially and/or for professional fishing tournaments.

A. Commercial Boat Haulers

Between 1993 and 1998, zebra mussels had been found on 18 vessels passing through California Agricultural Inspection stations. Some of these vessels were transported by commercial firms that either specialize in hauling boats or manufacturers of new vessels who haul used boats on their return trips. Although some firms require the hulls of boats they haul to be power washed, this practice is not universal. Even when followed, it may not be effective in removing all zebra mussels or other ANS present. Live organisms may remain on the hull and in crevices, bilges, bait wells, and cooling systems of motors. Component III will be supported through information and education, certification, and inspection programs.

The information and education program will involve locating and contacting commercial boat hauling firms. Through direct contact and follow up correspondence, the firms will be informed of the zebra mussel problem, alerted to the possibility that they may be transporting zebra mussels and other ANS to uninfested waters, and advised of what actions they can take to avoid this from occurring.

An ANS inspection training program will be established to teach employees of boat hauling firms how to properly inspect and clean boats and related equipment. Employees who successfully complete the training will receive a certificate. Hauling firms will be encouraged to have their employees complete the training program and to then begin implementing an inspection and cleaning program of all boats before they are hauled. Participating firms will be authorized to place a sticker on boats they haul, certifying the boat has been inspected for zebra mussels and other ANS.

B. Boats Hauled for Professional Fishing Tournaments

Numerous professional fishing tournaments are held around the country, resulting in boats being transported from one body of water to another, including those from zebra mussel infested to uninfested waters. Although some tournaments require participants to sign a statement that they are not carrying ANS, this requirement is spotty and often ineffective. Information, certification, and inspection programs could be implemented to help ensure that zebra mussels are not spread by those involved with professional fishing tournaments. State and tribal agencies will be encouraged to implement tournament regulations addressing the transport of ANS.

As part of the information program, material about zebra mussels and other ANS issues will be available at fishing tournaments. Tournament organizers will be contacted and informed about the zebra mussel problem and how they can help prevent their spread in 100th meridian jurisdictions and west. Until an official inspection program is implemented, tournament organizers will be encouraged to ask participants to inspect their boats before the tournament begins.

An ANS inspection training program could be established to teach tournament representatives how to properly inspect and clean boats and equipment that will be used during the tournament. Representatives who successfully complete the training would receive a certificate. Tournament organizers would be encouraged to have their representatives complete the training program and to begin implementing an inspection and cleaning program of all boats before they participated in a tournament. Tournament participants who had their boats inspected would be authorized to place a sticker on the windshield of their boat certifying the boat had been inspected for zebra mussels and other ANS. Under this scenario, only boats with these stickers would be allowed to participate in the tournaments.

Tasks required to implement this component include:
1) Locate firms that haul boats commercially.
2) Contact those firms explaining the Initiative and requesting their participation.
3) Meet with representatives of firms to discuss the Initiative.
4) Develop a training program and train boat inspectors.
5) Develop and produce certification for inspectors.
6) Develop, reproduce, and disseminate inspection forms.
7) Develop a list of contacts for professional fishing tournaments.
8) Contact tournament organizers and inform them about the Initiative and encourage their participation.
9) Attend professional fishing tournaments.
10) Train and certify tournament representatives to inspect boats.
11) Contact State and tribal agencies and encourage them to address the transportation of zebra mussels and other ANS in their regulations.

Component IV
Monitoring

Objective: Establish monitoring sites on waters in the 100th meridian jurisdictions and west to determine if zebra mussels and other ANS are present.

A. Background

Although currently undetected, zebra mussels may have already spread west of the 100th meridian. Effective monitoring is important to ensure that if zebra mussels are present, they will be detected. Early identification of zebra mussel infestation can decrease their potential impact on native resources, manmade structures, and the economy. This component will expand upon current management activities of Federal water management agencies, the Service, States, electric utilities, and others. Monitoring protocol will be developed through a workshop represented by Federal, State, and private entities. The Service will coordinate efforts to monitor for the presence or absence of zebra mussels. Findings will be reported to the National Nonindigenous Aquatic Nuisance Species Information Center in Gainesville, Florida.

Water bodies in 100th meridian jurisdictions and west will be assessed by Federal and State agencies to determine their potential for zebra mussel infestation. Physical and chemical measurements will be evaluated using a standardized risk assessment protocol along with recreational use patterns. Maps of assessed sites will be provided to State resource agencies and high-risk waters will be monitored periodically.

Tasks required to implement this component include:
1) Develop a list of zebra mussel monitoring activities west of the 100th meridian.
2) Perform risk assessment of bodies of water west of the 100th meridian.
3) Develop maps indicating areas of high, medium, and low risk.
4) Monitor high-risk areas.

Component V
Rapid Response

Objective: Eradicate or contain zebra mussels immediately following detection.

A cooperative rapid response effort among government agencies and the private sector is required to contain zebra mussels once they are detected. Zebra mussel sightings must be confirmed by qualified entities (Marsden, 1992). Jurisdictions along the 100th meridian and west will be asked to identify points of contact for receiving and confirming reports and coordinating response activities. Jurisdictions will also be asked to establish rapid response teams.

Once a new zebra mussel infestation has been identified, the next most likely site of infestation will be determined. By reviewing watershed maps and recreational use patterns, sites that are likely to be invaded next will be identified.

A national containment and control plan will be developed through a workshop to identify techniques for controlling and eradicating zebra mussels. This program will include outreach to educate the public about where zebra mussels have been sighted and how their transfer from infested sites can be prevented. Individuals making up a response team will be trained to implement certain aspects of the containment and control plan if zebra mussel infestations are discovered in 100th meridian jurisdictions and west. Decisions will be made as to how to handle zebra mussel containment and control if they are found in large bodies of water in the West.

Tasks required to implement this component include:
1) Develop a response/containment plan.
2) Train response team.
3) Equip response team.
4) Implement response/containment plan when necessary.

Component VI
Identification and Risk Assessment of Additional Pathways

Objective: Establish a program to identify additional pathways by which zebra mussels and other ANS could become established west of the 100th meridian. Evaluate these pathways and develop an action plan for those having potential risks.

This component will involve the development and funding of a program for identifying pathways, other than those that are boating and personal watercraft related, by which zebra mussels and other ANS may become introduced west of the 100th meridian. A risk assessment for each pathway identified will be conducted and actions for risk reduction will be developed. Once specific action plans have been developed, the focus and funding will be directed toward implementation where feasible. Tasks required to implement this component are the same as the objective.

Component VII
Evaluation

Objective: Ensure the effectiveness of the 100th Meridian Initiative in preventing the westward spread of zebra mussels and other ANS.

As the Initiative evolves, a timely and comprehensive evaluation of the effectiveness of actions taken is required to respond to needed changes. An evaluation protocol will be developed to assess whether Initiative objectives have been and are being met. Deficiencies will be identified and, if required, modifications will be made.

Evaluations will be conducted by those who directly implement the Initiative. An annual meeting will be held of key personnel, including representatives from Federal, State, Provinces, Tribes, and private agencies, who are implementing the Initiative to discuss the results of the evaluation. An annual evaluation report will be prepared. Required changes to the Initiative will be incorporated, and ineffective actions will be eliminated.

Tasks required to implement this component include:
1) Develop assessment format and disseminate to key persons involved in implementing the Initiative.
2) Set up an annual meeting to evaluate the Initiative.
3) Develop an annual assessment of the Initiative and make necessary modifications.

IV. Operational Needs and Estimated Costs

The spread of zebra mussels and other ANS in the West will require a concerted long-term campaign. Consequently, implementation of the 100th Meridian Initiative will require a minimum of 5 years and approximately $5 million. First year's start up costs will be higher than projected costs for the following years. Cost breakdowns for each Initiative component for the 5-year program are identified in the "Operational Needs and Estimated Costs" table. The projected costs for this Initiative are but a fraction of the economic impact that zebra mussels will inflict if they invade and become established in western waters.

Operational Needs and Estimated Costs Table

Tasks and associated costs required for implementing the 100th Meridian Initiative.

Component I: Information and Education	Participants	Year 1	Year 2	Year 3	Year 4	Year 5
Task 1: Complete development of a theme, brochure, poster, and sticker describing the Initiative (completed)	USFWS Boat/U.S. BPA					
Task 2: Print 500,000 brochures	USFWS	$50,000				
Task 3: Produce 2,500 posters	USFWS	$1,875				
Task 4: Produce 100,000 stickers	USFWS	$500				
Task 5: Place and replenish brochures and posters at visitor centers, weigh stations, and rest areas west of the Mississippi River	USFWS	$5,000	$1,000	$1,000	$1,000	$1,000
Task 6: Produce and erect billboards to be used on 11 highway corridors	USFWS Manitoba ND, SD, NE KS, OK, TX	$25,000	$22,000	$22,000	$22,000	$22,000
Task 7: Develop and print a zebra mussel advisory sign	USFWS	$10,000				
Task 8: Post zebra mussel advisory signs at public boat access sites west of the Mississippi River	Jurisdictions west of the MS River	$3,600				
Task 9: Create TV and radio public information spots on preventative messages including inspections	USFWS Sea Grant	$10,000	$10,000	$2,000		
Task 10: Broadcast spots on radio and TV	USFWS	$10,000	$10,000	$10,000	$10,000	$10,000
Task 11: Attend boating and sportfishing shows to advertise the Initiative	USFWS Sea Grant States	$15,000	$15,000	$15,000	$15,000	$15,000
Task 12: Place Initiative information in State boater registration packages and fishing regulations when feasible	100th meridian jurisdictions and those west					
Task 13: Develop articles for newspapers and magazines	USFWS Sea Grant States Provinces					
Subtotals		$130,975	$58,000	$50,000	$48,000	$48,000

14

Component II: Voluntary boat inspections and boater surveys	Participants	Year 1	Year 2	Year 3	Year 4	Year 5
Task 1: Develop standard inspection procedures	USFWS Manitoba ND, SD, NB, KS, OK, TX	$10,000	$2,000			
Task 2: Hire and train boat inspectors	USFWS States	$109,000	$252,000	$504,000	$504,000	$504,000
Task 3: Develop, reproduce, and disseminate inspection and survey forms	USFWS	$200	$100	$50	$50	$50
Task 4: Submit completed forms to USFWS	USFWS MB, ND, SD, NB, KS, OK, TX	$36	$36	$36	$36	$36
Subtotals		**$119,236**	**$254,136**	**$504,086**	**$504,086**	**$504,086**

Component III: Commercially hauled boats	Participants	Year 1	Year 2	Year 3	Year 4	Year 5
Task 1: Locate firms that haul boats commercially	USFWS	$20,000	$20,000	$20,000	$20,000	$20,000
Task 2: Contact those firms explaining the Initiative and requesting their participation						
Task 3: Meet with representatives of firms to discuss the Initiative						
Task 4: Develop training program for boat inspectors	USFWS					
Task 5: Develop and produce certification for inspectors	USFWS				$1,500	
Task 6: Develop, reproduce and disseminate inspection forms	USFWS				$150	$50
Task 7: Develop a list of contacts for professional fishing tournaments	USFWS	$4,000				
Task 8: Contact tournament organizers and inform them about the Initiative and encourage their participation	USFWS	$5,000	$2,000			
Task 9: Attend professional fishing tournaments	USFWS States west of the MS River	$10,000	$10,000	$10,000	$10,000	$10,000
Task 10: Train and certify tournament representatives to inspect boats	USFWS					
Task 11: Contact State and tribal agencies and encourage them to address the transportation of zebra mussels and other ANS in their regulations	USFWS	$10,000	$7,000	$5,000	$5,000	$5,000
Subtotals		**$49,000**	**$39,000**	**$35,000**	**$36,650**	**$35,050**

Component IV: Monitoring	Participants	Year 1	Year 2	Year 3	Year 4	Year 5
Task 1: Develop a list of zebra mussel monitoring activities west of the 100th meridian	USFWS	$7,000				
Task 2: Perform risk assessments of bodies of water west of the 100th meridian	USFWS BOR, Corps BLM, States, Power Co.	$250,000	$175,000	$100,000		
Task 3: Develop maps indicating areas of high, low, and medium risk	USFWS	$30,000	$80,000	$50,000		
Task 4: Monitor high-risk areas	USFWS BOR, Corps BLM, Tribes States, Provinces, Power Co.	$350,000	$350,000	$350,000	$350,000	$350,000
Subtotals		**$637,000**	**$605,000**	**$500,000**	**$350,000**	**$350,000**
Component V: Rapid Response						
Task 1: Develop a response/containment plan	USFWS BOR, BLM Tribes, States Provinces	$10,000				
Task 2: Train response team	USFWS	$50,000				
Task 3: Equip response team	USFWS	$100,000				
Task 4: Implement response/containment plan when necessary	USFWS	$30,000	$30,000	$30,000	$30,000	$30,000
Subtotals		**$190,000**	**$30,000**	**$30,000**	**$30,000**	**$30,000**
Component VI: Identification and risk assessment of additional pathways	USFWS BOR BLM States Provinces	$10,000 $10,000 $10,000	$10,000 $10,000 $10,000	$10,000 $10,000 $10,000	$10,000 $10,000 $10,000	$10,000 $10,000 $10,000
Subtotals		**$30,000**	**$30,000**	**$30,000**	**$30,000**	**$30,000**
Component VII: Evaluation						
Task 1: Develop assessment format and disseminate to key persons involved in implementing the Initiative	USFWS	$1,000				
Task 2: Set up annual meeting to evaluate the Initiative	USFWS	$3,000	$3,000	$3,000	$3,000	$3,000
Task 3: Develop an annual assessment of the Initiative and make necessary modifications	USFWS BOR, BLM States, Provinces	$5,000	$5,000	$5,000	$5,000	$5,000
Subtotals		**$9,000**	**$8,000**	**$8,000**	**$8,000**	**$8,000**
Grand Totals		**$1,165,211**	**$1,024,136**	**$1,157,086**	**$1,006,736**	**$1,005,136**

Appendix

100th Meridian Initiative to Prevent the Westward Spread of Zebra Mussel

Comments

Comments

TRAILERED BOAT SURVEY INTERVIEW FORM

Interviewer:_____Date:_____Time:_____am/pm

Location: _____

Type of Survey: Contact____ Observe____

Where From?

Purpose of Transport: Commercial ____   Personal ____

Other (explain) _____

Home State: _____ Zip Code: _____ Boat Number:_____
Trailer Tag: _____

How often has this boat been launched this year? _____

Do you remember where (you launched most recently)?

Water body 1_____
State: _____ County: _____

Water body 2_____
State: _____ County: _____

Water body 3_____
State: _____ County: _____

Water body 4_____
State: _____ County: _____

Where are you going?   Do you have a definite destination?
Do you know where you are going to launch next?

Water body 1 _____ State: _____

Water body 2 _____ State: _____

Information Exchange: Viewed ____ Read _____Brochures Accepted _____

Results of boat inspection

Rejected: _____   Inspected: _____

Results	Zebra Mussels	Still Alive?	Any Vegetation?	Other Exotics	Action Taken
Boat Deck	_____	_____	_____	_____	_____
Boat Hull	_____	_____	_____	_____	_____
Bilge, bait wells	_____	_____	_____	_____	_____
Motor	_____	_____	_____	_____	_____
Trailer	_____	_____	_____	_____	_____
Fishing/other equip.	_____	_____	_____	_____	_____
Other	_____	_____	_____	_____	_____

100th Meridian Initiative to Prevent the Westward Spread of Zebra Mussel

TRAILERED BOAT SURVEY INTERVIEW SHORT FORM

Lake _____ Park _____ Date _____

1. Home state _____ ZIP Code _____

2. Where was the boat used last?

Name of last water body _____

State: _____

Number of days: _____

Name of second to last water body _____

State: _____

Number of days: _____

3. Boat was last used _____ (days) ago.

4. Destination from this lake/park _____ _____ (state)

5. Have you ever heard of zebra mussels?   Yes   No

6. Have zebra mussels ever been attached to your boat?   Yes   No

7. Do you remove vegetation from your boat & trailer
   after loading the boat?   Yes   No

Have information describing zebra mussels and Eurasian watermilfoil available for distribution.

References

California Department of Food and Agriculture, personal communication.

Cohen, A., A. Weinstein. 1998. The potential distribution and abundance of zebra mussels in California Dreissena, Volume 9, #1, May 1998, pages 1, 2, and 3.

Dreissena, Volume 9, #1, May 1998, The 100th Meridian Initiative introduction, page 4.

Fish Futures, Inc. 1994. Zebra mussel survey of boaters and inspection of boats, summer 1994, border crossings and other key sites, Manitoba watershed, Dwight Williamson, Manitoba Environment, Winnepeg, Manitoba, Canada, page 10 (unpublished report).

Indiana Department of Natural Resources discussion with staff.

Karnaukhov, V. N., and A. V. Karnuakhov. 1993. Perspectives on the ecological impacts of the zebra mussel *(Dreissena polymorpha)* in the former USSR and in North America, pages 729-731 from Nalepa, T. F. and D. W. Schloesser, Editors, Zebra mussels: biology, impacts and controls, page 810 and from Tyus, H., P. Dwyer, and S. Whitmore, 1993. Zebra mussels: Feasibility of preventing further invasion of the zebra mussel into the western United States, page 9.

Machie, G. L. 1989. Biology of the zebra mussel *(Dreissena polymorpha)* and observations of mussel colonization on unionid bivalves in Lake St. Clair of the Great Lakes from Nalepa, T. F., D. W. Schloesser, Editors, Zebra mussels: Biology, impacts, and control, pages 153 and 162.

Machie, G. L., W. N. Gibbons, B. W. Muncaster, and I. M. Gray. 1989. The zebra mussel, Dreissena polymorpha: A synthesis of European experiences and a preview of North America. Water Resources Branch, Great Lakes Section, Ontario Ministry of the Environment, London, Ontario, page 76 and appendices from Marsden, J. E., Standard protocols for monitoring and sampling zebra mussels, page 4.

Marsden, J. E. 1992. Standard protocols for monitoring and sampling zebra mussels, pages 2, 3, and 4.

McMahon, R. F., T. A. Ussery, and M.. Clarke. 1993. Use of immersion as a zebra mussel control method, Department of Biology, University of Texas at Arlington. Prepared for the U.S. Corps of Engineers, contract EL-93-1, page 33 from Tyus, H., P. Dwyer, and S. Whitmore, Zebra mussel feasibility of preventing further invasion of the zebra mussel into the western United States, page 9.

Miller, A. C., B. S. Payne, and R. F. McMahon. 1992. The zebra mussel: biology, ecology, and recommended control strategies, U.S. Army Corps of Engineers, Waterways Experiment Station, Publications E-92-1, Vicksburg, MS, page 5 from Tyus, H., P. Dwyer, and S. Whitmore, Zebra mussel feasibility of preventing further invasion of the zebra mussel into the western United States, page 9.

Nalepa, T. F., and D. W. Schloesser, editors. 1993. Zebra mussels: biology, impacts, and control. Lewis publishers, Boca Raton, Florida, page 810 from Tyus, H., P. Dwyer, and S. Whitmore, Zebra mussels: Feasibility of preventing further invasion of the zebra mussel into the western United States, pages 8 and 9.

National Park Service information, Glen Canyon National Recreational Area.

New York Sea Grant Extension Fact Sheet 1994. Don't pick up hitchhikers! Stop the zebra mussel!, 1994.

O'Neill, C. R. Jr. 1995. Economic impact of zebra mussels: The 1995 national zebra mussel information clearinghouse study, pages 1 and 2.

O'Neill, C. R. Jr. 1996. The zebra mussel: Impacts and control, pages 11, 12, 13, 14, and 17.

Schloesser, D. W., and W. P. Kovalak. 1991. Infestation of unionids by *Dreissena polymorpha* in a power plant canal in Lake Erie. Journal of Shellfish Research 10(2):355-359 from Tyus, H., P. Dwyer, and S. Whitmore, Zebra Mussels: Feasibility of preventing further invasion of the zebra mussel into the western United States, page 10.

Sea Grant Great Lakes Network April 7, 1998. *Zebra mussels and other nonindigenous species.*

The 100th Meridian Initiative - Action Plan Draft, January 9, 1998.

Tyus, H., Dwyer, W. P., and Whitmore S. 1993. Zebra mussels: Feasibility of preventing further invasion of the zebra mussel into the western United States. Pages 9, 19, and 20.

USGS news release September 18, 1997. Zebra mussels are spreading rapidly, USGS reports.

U.S. Department of the Interior
U.S. Fish and Wildlife Service
1849 C Street, NW
Washington, DC 20240
1 800/344 WILD

http://www.fws.gov

February 2001

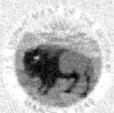